A Politics for the 99%

Marco Rosaire Conrad-Rossi

A Politics for the 99%

new-compass.net

A Politics for the 99%
2014 © Marco Rosaire Conrad-Rossi

ISBN 978-82-93064-32-9
ISBN 978-82-93064-33-6 (ebook)

Published by New Compass Press
Grenmarsvegen 12
N–3912 Porsgrunn
Norway

Design and layout by Eirik Eiglad
Cover illustration by Esben Slaatrem Titland

New Compass presents ideas on participatory democracy, social ecology, and movement building—for a free, secular, and ecological society.

New Compass is Camilla Svendsen Skriung, Sveinung Legard, Eirik Eiglad, Peter Munsterman, Kristian Widqvist, Lisa Roth, Camilla Hansen, Jakob Zethelius.

new-compass.net
2014

— Every political judgment helps to modify the facts on which it is passed. Political thought is itself a form of political action. Political science is the science not only of what is, but what ought to be.

E. H. Carr

Acknowledgments: I would like to thank Eirik Eiglad and Jakob Zethelius for making this pamphlet possible; Denise Bagget for editing early drafts of this pamphlet and moral support; Stephen Engelman, whose class in political philosophy inspired the initial arguments in this pamphlet; Simon Conrad-Rossi, who has always believed in me even when I have not; and Fulvia, whose pluck and kindness will build a better world.

The Occupy Wall Street demonstrations have had a transformative—and quite possibly a historical—effect on America's political discourse. The movement's main talking point, that they represent "the 99%" while a ruling "1%" runs the political economy, has become the first millennial political meme, and it has managed to change the entire parameters of debate around economic inequality. To discuss the divisions in Western societies as being cut along the lines of "workers" and "capitalists" is perhaps still taboo, and, to be perfectly honest, too inaccurate for explaining the totality of modern capitalism. However, the concept that there is a nebulous but very real "99%" that has been both victimized and neglected by the extravagance of a "1%" has resonated with people. It has tapped into their democratic and egalitarian impulses and has called people's attention to the absurdities of modern capitalism.

In the terms of inventing political memes that can capture the zeitgeist, Occupy Wall Street has been a success. That is undeniable. But, what is also undeniable is that in terms of forming a coherent and organized movement that could radically transform or even seriously challenge capitalism, Occupy Wall Street has been a failure. Just as quickly as it formed, it slid away. The language of Occupy Wall Street remains, but the movement itself has become directionless and self-destructive. Within a couple of months all of the encampments were gone and in a few years all the activism that it had inspired has dissipated. What is left of the Occupy Wall Street movement has degraded into cliques of conspiracy theorists, lifestyle radicals, and novice activists consumed with interpersonal dynamics.

Where did things go wrong?

It is tempting to write off the Occupy Wall Street movement completely, and indeed, many already have. However, this is a mistake. Throughout history social movements have come and gone, and each one, in its own unique way, offers insights into the processes of mass mobilization and the possibility for a better world. Occupy Wall Street is no different. No matter how damning its current manifestation is, its initial formation was quite unique and inspiring. There is a reason why today, even though there is very little left of the Occupy Wall Street movement, that leftwing pundits still refer to it with a sense of pining anticipation. There is still a hope that it could be revived or that something similar will come along and act as a springboard for the revolutionary change that so many people are hoping for. For this reason, the question is not why did Occupy Wall Street end up being such a failure, but why did the parts of Occupy Wall Street that were successful fail to succeed?

In order to answer this question it is necessary to decide which theoretical lens should be used to assess the Occupy Wall Street movement, and how this theory provides us with the tools for guiding the energy of the Occupy Wall Street movement into a more impactful direction. So far, the traditional revolutionary left has presented two options, Marxism and anarchism, both of which are problematic in their influence.

Since the 2007-2008 economic collapse, Marx and Marxism has experienced a revival. However, this new found appreciation for Marx and his acolytes has been more in the manner of spirit, a shared frustration and disgust with capitalism's primary characteristics, than a devotion to the actual specifics of Marx's theory. Many Occupy Wall Street encampments had "teach-ins" on the *Communist Manifesto*, but for the most part it was the *Manifesto's* "poetic" rather than its "scientific" aspects that resonated with participants.

Marx believed that the socialist revolution would be led by the industrial proletariat. Occupy Wall Street's main organizers are young students, many of which have had little experience in the factory life that Marx thought would discipline the working class. And, for many of them it is highly unlikely that they will ever work under factory conditions. Beyond the foresight of Marx, highly developed economies are seeing dramatic decreases in their manufacturing sectors. The expansion of financial markets, the growth of services sectors, and the development of certain global divisions of labor makes it highly unlikely that a substantial section of the working class will become proletarianized in the way that Marx predicted. This is not necessarily a bad thing. For decades, major theorists within the Left have challenged the hegemony of the industrial proletariat in the struggle for socialism. Long before industrialized economies developed into their modern postindustrial form, the factory was questioned as the primary loci of socialist struggles and new social spaces were recognized as legitimate terrains for battling capitalism. The Occupy Wall Street demonstrations show that action and theory are starting to converse with each other in this respect. The struggle against capitalism has started to take on a civic, and not just economic, character, where the collective reclaiming of public space exhibits a greater revolutionary potential than the mass strike.

In addition, Marx's belief that capitalism would experience its ultimate crisis through its own innovation has had little, if any, relevance for today's anti-capitalist radicals. In demonstrations like Occupy Wall Street the major concerns are not with automation displacing the working class but with the chaos unleashed on the economy as a whole through financial liberalization and the ecological consequences of market failures. Whatever benefits the variations of Marx's "crisis theory" of capitalism have had, the classical formulation that the introduction of new technologies would lead to a crisis of overproduction that would eventually desolate the working class, thus creating the impetus for rebellion, has not occurred. Nor does it seem likely it will ever occur. In highly developed economies, technological innovation has been almost entirely taken over by the State, and, under its guidance, is handed over to major corporations in the form of public-private partnerships. For developed nations, the social disjunctions created through industrialization have passed, and for developing nations these disjunctions take on a radically different meaning since they occur in the context of a global division of labor and a legacy of imperialism that did not exist in the nineteenth century European landscape where Marx developed his theories.

Finally—and most importantly—Marx believed that political consciousness formed as a product of class consciousness through the workers' experience of alienated labor. Ideas of alienated labor seem to have little relevance to the participants of Occupy Wall Street. Instead, the focus is on political consciousness as a product of political alienation itself. It is control over their government, and not that means of production, that people feel they have lost. The idea of workers seizing the means of production is recognized as a secondary concern to the idea of people seizing the means of social organization; the struggle against capitalism is not only about *what* decisions are being made about the economy, but also *how* those decisions are being made. The most unique aspect of the Occupy Wall Street encampments, the generally assemblies, were not formed purely for their strategic value, but as a means to psychologically reclaim a sense of lost power. They were formed with the intention of being a source of political virtue. The general assemblies were to provide examples of decision-making that genuinely embodied the ideals of democracy and at the same time exposed the "representative" democracy of Western governments as a charade.

The incompleteness of Marxist notions in describing Occupy Wall Street may make Marxism's major leftwing rival, anarchism, an attractive alternative for comprehending and directing the movement. However, this too is misguided. Anarchism's ability to guide any type of social movement has always been minimal. The reason is that anarchism, on its own, has never been a political movement, but rather a historical tendency. Nearly every major anarchist thinker has celebrated this aspect of the anarchist tradition, often claiming it as the embodiment of its non-dogmatic nature. However, righteous zeal against dogma can become its own dogma, and anarchists have consistently failed to offer any unified and coherent vision of what they do want once the State and capitalism have been abolished. The only way anarchists have ever made their ideas relevant is by modifying and attaching them to other social movements and concepts, such as mutualism, federalism, platformism, syndicalism and communism, in order to solidify and socialize the inherent vagueness and individualism of their ideas. Indeed, if Marxists have been accused of not having a sufficient theory of political power, often describing it as merely an extension of economic power in Marx's classic base-superstructure division, then anarchists have been equally guilty of having a mangled theory of social power, one that leads them to an explicit rejection of political power and a paranoid suspicion toward institutions, organization, and collective discipline in general.

A major problem with the Occupy Wall Street encampments was that they took too many of their cues from anarchism and this has contributed to the movement's current desultory state. The general assemblies were an attempt to reclaim a sense of lost power, but often this reclamation was for naught. In pursuit of a "non-dogmatic" approach to decision making, a dogmatic commitment to formal consensus or super-majorities for every decision was decided upon. This meant that power in the general assemblies remained individualized. Those individuals who had the greatest means to enforce their will were the ones who had the most time to attend meetings, and not the people who were the most collaborative or had the most reasonable proposals. In the pursuit of preserving individual autonomy, tiny minorities were able to control entire groups and prevented the developing and institutionalizing of the general assemblies into anything more than a venue to address people's most obvious and immediate concerns. Because of this, power never really transferred from individuals to the group as a whole. It stayed atomized within each individual. The general assemblies never became more than the sum of their parts.

Fortunately, there is another revolutionary theoretical lens for understanding and guiding movements like Occupy Wall Street. Communalism, a political philosophy that was being developed by Murray Bookchin after his break with anarchism, draws much on the ideas of Marxism and anarchism, but also attempts to breaks away from them. As of now, Communalism is in its infancy, but it has tremendous potential to eclipse both Marxism and anarchism by offering leftwing movements a radically new conception of politics. For Communalists, politics is the creation of social legitimacy through collective dialogue, and not through the use of organized violence in the form of hierarchical institutions. In this way, political power and democratic governance are nearly interchangeable terms. Politics is both the description and the realization of democracy. This means that the establishing of a libertarian socialist society requires an embracing of directly democratic governments that are in open opposition to States. In a flipping of both Marxist and anarchist notion of politics, Communalists believe that political power needs to be seized, but it needs to be seized not through States but in order to abolish States.

To help unravel these issues this pamphlet will offer an analysis of both Marx's and Bakunin's theory of the State and demonstrate that both believed that politics was a "necessary evil" of the State. For them political power was essentially a form of collective violence that exists outside of society, that intervenes in it, and that will "wither away" or be abolished with the end of class divisions and material scarcity. The reason for these assumptions is that both Marx and Bakunin rooted their conception of politics in liberal social contract theories that understood government and society existing in a dualistic tension with each other. In contrast, Communalism is based on a classical *polis* understanding of politics. What Communalism adds to this ancient *polis* understanding of politics is a radical egalitarianism that sees a government of communal democracy, along with a humanistic and secular culture and a communist economy, as having the greatest prospect for unlocking humanity's full potential.

The relevancy of this discussion to the Occupy Wall Street movement is that it was the process of self-actualization through collective dialogue that made the Occupy Wall Street movement so meaningful for so many people. The emphasis on collective dialogue in the general assemblies is what made the Occupy Wall Street movement so unique and important. No matter how mangled in practice, there was a general agreement among the participants of the Occupy Wall Street encampments that democracy was something that could be won only through its use, and it was the use of democracy, both direct and participatory, that would radicalize the movement. If this practice of self-actualization through collective dialogue that Communalism promotes, and that the Occupy Wall Street movement briefly exhibited, can be seized upon and institutionalized, then it is possible to birth another generation of leftwing radicals that could successfully push humanity into a better future.

Theories of the State: Marxism and Anarchism

To understand Marx's theory of the State it is first necessary to understand what Marx understood as the conditions for full human emancipation. Marx's emphasis on the productive forces in society interwove the two forms of oppression that he believed hindered the development of humanity: exploitation and material scarcity. Freedom was only possible in a society that was both classless and had material abundance. His disdain for rural living—which he referred to as "idiotic" in the *Communist Manifesto*, despite its often cooperative traditions—came from a recognition that though independent communal peasants were free of one form of oppression, that of exploitation, they were trapped by their inability to reach a state of material abundance. It mattered very little that property was held in common in such societies because the commonality of property essentially meant a commonality of poverty. With this in mind, the appearance of the State, and with it a social division of labor, was essentially a progressive step forward, out of primitive communism—the communism of shared poverty. It brought in the potential for greater material abundance through a division of labor, though at the costs of a new social structure stratified by class tensions.

For Marx, the State begins with the separation of the individual from the community, a separation that occurs only after material abundance has reached a level where the rift between individual and community is possible without threatening both. In this separation the advancement of the individual cannot occur without the detriment to the community and vice versa. This contradiction is institutionalized and "takes an independent form as the *State*, divorced from the real interests of the individual and the community, and at the same time as an illusory communal life, always based, however, on the real ties existing in every family and tribal conglomeration."[1] In this "illusory communal life," the interests of the dominant class become the "general interest" of all members of society. For the masses below, these "general interests" are "imposed on them as an interest 'alien' to them, and 'independent' of them, as in its turn a particular, peculiar 'general' interest."[2] The "illusory" aspect of the State's "illusory communal life" creates a sense of political estrangement, the feeling that one's political system is an alien force in one's own existence. Thus the State, as an intervening force in society, always intervenes on the behalf of a particular class while claiming a universal intervention on behalf of all citizens.

There are several important points to take away in Marx's conception of the State and political power. First, though the State is ultimately a regressive force, Marx believed that there were many opportunities where the State could play a progressive role depending on historical circumstances. The most important of these was in the battle against capitalism. The State could be used to smash the bourgeoisie under the dictatorship of the proletariat. The rise of working class political power meant the destruction of the State as an "illusory communal life," by making it into an *actual* communal life. This is so because the working class—being the majority—is able to "represent its interest in turn as the general interest"[3] and therefore can reconcile the contradiction between the State as a universal and the State as a tool of a particular class.

Marx's belief that the State could potentially be a progressive democratic force is best explained by Robert M. Cutler's interpretation of Marx's own theory of the democracy. Cutler explains that for Marx "the essence of the State was Democracy itself; he conceived Democracy to be embodied in a constitution hierarchically superior to other political forms, and therefore concluded that the State had to be *realized* to its highest degree."[4] Culter's interpretation is supported by Marx's early criticisms of Hegel. Democracy, Marx asserted in his critique of Hegel's *Philosophy of Right*, was politics trying to realize itself within the State. Democracy was for Marx the State no longer in contradiction with itself, or as he put it, "democracy is the solved *riddle* of all constitutions."⁵The reason that the riddle is "solved" is because the dialectic between the ruler and the ruled is resolved. As Marx observed, in a democratic State, "not merely *implicitly* and in essence but *explicitly* in reality, the constitution is constantly brought back to its actual basis, the *actual human being*, the *actual people*, and established as the people's *own* work. The constitution appears as what it is, a free product of man."⁶

The second point is that even though Marx believed in the principle that democracy was the realization of the State—and that the dictatorship of the proletariat would be the most democratic State known to history—he was extremely ambiguous as to what form the dictatorship of the proletariat would take. His notion of the dictatorship of the proletariat was always structurally vague and it vacillated between extremes. At times, he favored a highly centralized version of the dictatorship of the proletariat. In the *Communist Manifesto*, Marx clearly states that the immediate goals of communists should be the "centralization of credit in the hands of the State, by means of a national bank with State capital and an exclusive monopoly" and the "centralization of the means of communication and transport in the hands of the State."⁷ However, during the height of the Paris Commune, Marx changed his tune. With the Paris Commune as the example, he praised a decentralized form of workers' government, and advocated for "revolutionary workers' governments, whether in the form of municipal committees and municipal councils or in the form of workers' clubs and workers' committees."⁸

Even more confusing is his tendency to view communism as developing peacefully in societies that had republican forms of government. He suggested that the struggle of the working class was uniquely different in countries like the United States, England, and possibly Holland, where a degree of democratic rights had been won. There, socialism could be achieved through legal channels. At the same time, he would declare that the forms of government were trivial in the context of class struggle, modes of production, and the inevitable violent overthrow of capitalism; in other words, democratic rights were important except when they were not.

The stark difference between these positions is difficult to reconcile, and it demonstrates a confused political philosophy on the part of Marx. Marx may have been a democrat in spirit, but he lacked a sufficient praxis of democracy, and this led to numerous contradictions in his work. For example, though he praised the Paris Commune for transforming the old centralized French bureaucracy into a working class government, a "self-government of the producers,"[9] he also praised its potential "to be a working, not a parliamentary body, executive and legislative at the same time."[10] The consolidation of executive and legislative functions into a single entity is the type of thing that makes more sophisticated democratic theorists howl. Democratic governments can only function when there is a clear separation of powers. Mixing these two functions, not to mention leaving out completely the importance of a judiciary, means that responsibility for creating policies eventually falls to a handful of administrators and technicians rather than the population as a whole.[11] Frustratingly, the only thing truly consistent in Marx's political writings is the vagueness of his democratic ideals.

The third point is that Marx's conception of political power is that it is a form of collectivized violence; that is, it is a repressive form of power. Despite its emancipatory goals, the dictatorship of the proletariat is no exception to the principle of politics as essentially organized violence. What makes the dictatorship of the proletariat unique is that it is supposed to be the final reign of repression before a new utopia. Violent repression can be justified if it is synchronized with other progressive elements of history. As explained by Engels, political violence "is the midwife of every old society pregnant with a new one ... that it is the instrument with the aid of which social movement forces its way through and shatters the dead, fossilized political forms."[12]

This view of the State as a potentially revolutionary but always violent institution further complicates Marx's statement on the possibility for peaceful revolutions in nations with republican governments. Even if the working class were to come to power through electoral means, its use of State power would be a violent act of repression. The point was made clear by Lenin. What Lenin saw as Marx's main objection to the anarchists was not the wrongness of their theories, but that their anti-statist rhetoric served to disarm the working class, both figuratively and literally, of their historical role in overthrowing capitalism. For Lenin, what Marx "did oppose was the proposition that the workers should renounce the use of arms, organized violence, *that is, the state*, which is to serve to 'crush the resistance of the bourgeoisie.'"[13] In this sense, the "peacefulness" of electoral socialism lies only in the means that the working class uses to come to power, not in how that power would be used to transform society. For that change a certain degree of violence would always be necessary.

The final point is Marx's view of the apolitical nature of a communist society. To understand fully how Marx came to this perspective it is necessary to reexamine his idea that freedom springs forth from the historical end of both exploitation and material scarcity. Marx establishes his material conception of history—between his base (economics) and his superstructure (everything else)—upon what he considered to be the ongoing social problem of history: the conquest of the "realm of necessity" in order to establish the "realm of freedom." Both animals and humans engaged in what Marx referred to as "life-activity"—the satisfaction of subsistence. What Marx found important is that humans are able to transform life-activity into labor-activity through the application of their subjective agency onto an objective nature. For Marx, animals are "immediately identical" to the natural world. They have no subjective agency (or at least not to the degree that people have it). Humanity, in contrasts, is able to understand itself separate from nature, and in this separateness can transform nature into the products of society.

According to Marx it is in this process of transforming nature into the products of society that the struggle for human freedom is fought. Economics is the "base" in the Marxist construction of social change, not because economics is all that matters, but because nothing can matter without first conquering the "realm of need," that is, satiating the means for subsistence. For Marx, the "realm of freedom" "actually begins only where labour which is determined by necessity and mundane considerations ceases; thus in the very nature of things it lies beyond the sphere of actual material production."[14] In *The German Ideology,* Marx discusses how under communism it is "possible for me to do one thing today and another tomorrow, to hunt in the morning, fish in the afternoon, rear cattle in the evening, criticize after dinner, just as I have a mind, without ever becoming hunter, fisherman, shepherd or critic."[15] This multitude of labor activities is only possible when there are appropriate conditions that allow for the "necessity and mundane considerations" of labor activity to end. People no longer pursue them out of the requirements for subsistence, but out of their own sense of agency.

What is of interest in these activities is what Marx does not include. If we are to hunt in the morning, then why not debate in the afternoon, propose a piece of legislation in the evening, and vote on a measure after dinner. The reason is that there is no need. For Marx, a communist society would be an openly apolitical, if not antipolitical, one. Humanity derives its sense of agency through the governing of things—that is the production of commodities through the liberation of self-realized labor—not through the inherent sociability of society and the governing of each other. The workers' State only exists as a necessity for dismantling capitalist relations. Once those relations are gone, the dictatorship of the proletariat has no historical or social purpose. With the material conditions for freedom met the need for politics evaporates. The dictatorship of the proletariat and its political power "withers away." There is no longer a need for an alien force to intervene in society because the alienation of society from itself breaks down through the development of communism.

In all fairness to Marx the apolitical nature of communism is rooted in a utopian impulse. As explained above, Marx believed that political power was always a violent and repressive affair; all governments are "necessary evils" whose evilness only exists as a matter of historical circumstances. The desire to liberate humanity from all forms of oppression under communism necessitated the liberation also from politics. As Erich Fromm recognized, Marx's belief in the necessity of a violent revolutionary State in the overthrow of capitalism is a sign of his humanism; he limited this force to a transitory phase rather than glorifying it as an eternal feature of society. According to Fromm, Marx "did *not* believe in the creative power of force, in the idea that political force itself could create a new social order. For this reason, force, for Marx, could have at most only a transitory significance, never the role of a permanent element in the transformation of society."[16]

Marx's theory of the State has two problems. One of which was corrected by anarchism, and the other which was made worse by anarchism. In contrast to Marx, Bakunin understood the State to be an inherently regressive force in society. Its "progressive" nature is only evident when it is compared to the "primitive bestiality" that preceded it. For Bakunin the State was an extension, rather than a form of transcendence, of the savagery of tribal living. For each horror of tribal life, Bakunin saw a parallel in modern Europe. Tribalism had been replaced with patriotism; local priests replaced with intellectuals; cannibalism replaced with war and exploitation; and of course, the tribal god with the Church. For this reason, the State could not be effectively seized in a socialist revolution, but had to be smashed. For Marx the political revolution was a "necessary evil" to abolish capitalism and would "wither away" with the triumphant realization of communism; for Bakunin the political revolution was the place where the social revolution goes to die.

The belief that the State was a new "god" figured heavily into Bakunin's analysis. In Bakunin's mind the State was the "younger brother" of the Church. Unlike Marx, who saw the modern State being brought about by the French Revolution and the rise of the bourgeoisie, Bakunin placed the birth of the modern State at the beginning of the Reformation. With the power of the Church in decline, the State rose as an alternative means for maintaining inequalities and hierarchy. In this way, Bakunin saw his own anarchism as a logical extension of atheism. For Bakunin, a sincere denial of the authority of religion would eventually lead all able thinkers to a denial of political authority. Just as scientific laws had replaced the need for theology, social customs and natural laws would replace the need for legislation and constitutions.

The important point of this analysis is that Bakunin understood the State as a means of creating classes and hierarchy, and not simply a means to maintain a class structure that had already evolved through historical modes of production. For him, the bourgeoisie were to be resisted not merely because they were the class of exploitation—though exploitation was an obvious concern for Bakunin—but because they were the class that was in control of the State.

The main division in society was not between the working class and capitalists, but between the working class and the political classes:

> The State has always been the patrimony of some privileged class: a priestly class, an aristocratic class, a bourgeois class. And finally, when all the other classes have exhausted themselves, the State then becomes patrimony of the bureaucratic class and then falls—or, if you will, rises—to the position of a machine. But in any case it is absolutely necessary for the salvation of the State that there should be some privileged class devoted to its preservation.[17]

In essence, what Bakunin added to Marx was a critique of bureaucracy and its ability to create class structures through hierarchical forms of social organization. Marx was in principle a centralist. Despite his revisions after the Paris Commune, Marx favored centralizing the means of production within the nation-State as a way to eliminate both capitalist modes of production and the scattered forms of feudal power throughout Europe. He supported nationalist struggles strategically and partially, always fearful that they could break up larger political units. He believed that the unification of humanity within a single centralized authority was a progressive and natural tendency of civilization, one that would eventually happen without a reliance on external coercion. For him, the State's repressive mechanism would slowly deteriorate as the tools of governance were consolidated into a political core of intellectuals guided solely by their own reason.

Lenin's notion of "democratic centralism" is the political expression of this general faith in centralization without coercion. In response to critics of the expansion of the Bolshevik bureaucracy, Lenin was quick to reply that the bureaucracy was necessary in a largely rural country like Russia. According to Lenin, once the peasants were brought into the industrial sphere and true socialism was established, the bureaucracy would slowly wither away because society would have the material and intellectual means to govern itself. Similarly, during the Cuban Revolution, Che Guevara argued that centralization was the greatest means for eliminating the bureaucracy within the Cuban State. According to Guevara "from the standpoint of objective analysis, it is obvious that there will be less bureaucracy the more centralized are enterprises or production units recording and controlling operations. If every enterprise could centralize all its administrative activities, its bureaucracy would be reduced to a small nucleus of unit directors plus someone to collect information for headquarters."[18] These arguments seem self-serving for those in positions of power, but they are not without their theoretical justification. They flow logically from aspects of Marx's own analysis.

In contrast, Bakunin was a federalist. He believed in allowing small political units a degree of autonomy over their own affairs, while a larger body set the general parameters for action. He supported national movements for self-determination and ethnic minorities (with the notable exception of the Jews) under the conviction that the breakup of the nation-State could only lead to the federation of a "commune of communes." In both his *Revolutionary Catechism* and speech before the League of Peace and Freedom, Bakunin set a detailed description of this federalist model which included "the free federation of individuals into communes, of communes into provinces, of the provinces into nations, and, finally, of the nations into the United States of Europe first, and the entire world eventually."[19]

For advocates of democracy, Bakunin's federalism is more appealing than Marx's centralism. History has shown that federated or confederated institutions have been more supportive of freedom than a perpetual drive toward centralization. But, Bakunin's federalism poses a theoretical problem; it runs completely counter to his anarchism. For Bakunin revolutionary socialism could "succeed only through the development and organization of the nonpolitical or antipolitical social power."[20] The social revolution was "diametrically opposed" to a political one[21] and should lead to a "reduction in political action in favor of the liberty of social life."[22] According to Bakunin, the apolitical nature of a socialist future could only be possible if current revolutionary forces took on an antipolitical nature. In 1849, after Bakunin participated in a wave of insurrections throughout Central Europe, he proudly proclaimed, "I believe neither in constitutions nor in laws; the best constitution possible would not satisfy me. We need nothing less than the bursting-out-into-life of a new world, lawless and therefore free."[23] His entire critique of the State is dependent on the elimination of political laws, and with it, acts of legislation and adjudication, and replacing them with natural and social laws based on economic management and social customs.

However, when it came to facing the actual problems of Europe—especially the problems of world peace and

European unification—Bakunin drops the "bursting-out-into-life" rhetoric and appears more as a cautious advocate for global government than the revolutionary anarchist he was known to be. In his *Revolutionary Catechism*, Bakunin calls for "provincial parliaments," which must act in accordance with a "Charter of the Federation of Communes." His agenda includes "International Tribunals" that are beyond appeal and tasked with resolving conflicts between communes in order to avoid the outbreak of war. He also wants an "International Parliament" that will make decisions on behalf of all communes. This is hardly the project of a man who believes "neither in constitutions nor in laws."

In order to square this peculiar circle in Bakunin's thought Sam Dolgoff has qualified Bakunin's *Revolutionary Catechism* by framing it as a set of bold reforms in order to transition capitalist society into an anarchist one. He explains that "the *Revolutionary Catechism* does not attempt to picture the perfect anarchist society—the anarchist heaven. Bakunin had in mind a society in transition toward anarchism. The building of a full-fledge anarchist society is the work of future generations."[24] The problem with this interpretation is that it contradicts the consensus among scholars of Bakunin that he refused to accept any transitional phase toward anarchism. In the preface to Sam Dolgoff own collection on Bakunin's writings, anarchist historian Paul Avrich clearly writes that "Bakunin was a firm believer in immediate revolution. He rejected the view that revolutionary forces will emerge gradually, in the fullness of time. What he demanded, in effect, was 'freedom now.' He would countenance no temporizing with the existing system.... Gradualism and reformism in any shape futile, palliatives and compromises of no use."[25] Similarly, Robert M. Cutler, in his introduction to his own Bakunin anthology writes that for Bakunin, "social emancipation did not exist in degrees; either it existed or it did not."[26] The truth of the matter is that anarchists have been correct to point out Marx's contradictory, if not latent authoritarianism, concerning the dictatorship of the proletariat. However, in doing so they have failed to realize that Bakunin, and their own anarchist tradition, is just as guilty as Marx in offering an inconsistent view of political power.

Pure anarchism has never been—nor will it ever be—a political project. Anarchism has only reached any significance as a political movement when it has augmented its rejection of all forms of political authority with a constructive program that is willing to give a degree of credence to some new form of politics, often a partial or mangled form. For Proudhon and Bakunin this was federalism, for Kropotkin it was village communes, for Makhno it was rural communism and platformism, for Rocker it was syndicalism. This is an extremely problematic aspect of the anarchist tradition. As Murray Bookchin has pointed out:

> Accordingly, anarchists have long regarded every *government* as a *state* and condemned it accordingly—a view that is a recipe for the elimination of *any* organized social life whatever. While the *state* is the instrument by which an *oppressive* and *exploitative* class regulates and coercively controls the behavior of an exploited class by a ruling class, a *government*—or better still, a *polity*—is an ensemble of institutions designed to deal with the problems of consociational life in an orderly and hopefully fair manner … Annoying as it must seem to Marxists

and anarchists alike, the cry for a *constitution*, for a responsible and responsive government, and ever for *law* or *nomos* has been clearly articulated … by the oppressed for centuries against the capricious rule exercised by monarchs, nobles, and bureaucrats.[27]

Bookchin is quoted at length because his comments get to the heart of the matter. What Bookchin shows is that the debate on political power that has divided Marxists and anarchists for over a century and a half is an argument over a misunderstood issue. Both sides are attacking the same problem, but from two different angles, each with a certain merit to their perspective, and each with a faulty set of theoretical tools.

The best example of this is found in Bakunin's own comments on the parallels between various utopian forms of the State and the abolition of the State. He wrote that "the worldwide State, or rather the People's State of which the German Communists speak, can therefore mean only one thing: *the abolition of the state*."[28] Bakunin makes such a statement thinking he has the German communist (Marx and company) beat, but the problem is also Bakunin's own. By equating the abolition of the State with the "People's State" or even the "worldwide State," he gives weight to Marx's argument that there is something about political power that cannot be ignored in the socialist revolution. Ironically, the abolition of the State, and Marx's realization of the State as the fullest expression of democracy (the "People's State") and the unification of the world into a universal political system (the "worldwide State") are all really saying the same thing. Despite that each is using language that makes the other position impossible, each proposal is addressing a different form of oppression that humans seek liberation from—whether it is isolationism, parochialism, or social hierarchies. This recognition requires that we admit that freedom is a multifaceted affair where the escape from one form of oppression can easily drive a society into another. Combined the argument for all these States and against all States is saying that the political power within the State is needed and desirable as a self-organizing tool for society. Political power itself is a way for humans to escape personal isolation by the creation of a public life. However, the idea that politics is a form of hierarchically organized collective violence, an alien force outside of society that obtrusively intervenes within it, must be done away with—abolished—if society and the individuals within it are to be truly free.

Social Contract Theory: Its Influence and Problems

In constructing their own theories of political power, both Marxism and anarchism have been greatly influenced by liberalism, specifically the tradition of social contract theorists that dominated much of the political philosophy just prior to Marx and Bakunin. Both Marx and Bakunin had a mixed relationship with social contract theory. They were highly critical of certain assumptions—with Bakunin having a special hatred for Rousseau—while at the same time willing to accept others. It is not the point of this pamphlet to explain the entire cannon of social contract theorists, or to highlight the importance of those figures that produced work prior to Marx and Bakunin. Rather, this pamphlet will outline common assumptions of social contract theorists in political philosophy and show how Marx and Bakunin both rejected and accepted these assumptions.

Generally speaking, all social contract theorists share four axioms on the relationship between humans and society. First, people can be understood as individuals existing in a pre-social "state of nature" or "original position" where they have perfect liberty. Second, when individuals commune— that is, when they move from individuals to social beings— conflict inevitably arises, and there is a need to minimize these conflicts by sacrificing a degree of liberty to ensure one's security. Third, this security is enforced by a "social contract" that has two elements. The first is a horizontal element that establishes the rights and duties that each member in society has to one another, and the second is a vertical element which establishes the rights and duties that government and society have to each other.[29] Four, politics is a realm of force. Government is the enforcer of the horizontal social contract between members of the society, and the vertical contract between government and society is maintained through the threat of violent revolution. Marx and Bakunin rejected the first two axioms, but to a large degree they accepted the latter two.

The emergence of socialist theory reoriented the social sciences from the individual to society, and, in doing so, individuality itself became recognized as a social creation. This had intellectual as well as moral implications. Intellectually, individuals were seen as products of their environment. The timeless soul of Christianity—and with it free will and responsibility—became subsumed into the more earthly conceptions of humanity as contingent on historical forces. Freedom for the individual was to be understood as a social affair. It was not possible for an individual to be free unless that individual lived in a free society. The reason this is so is because, despite what social contract theorists say, no one voluntarily enters into society. We are all born into a social setting, a family, a community, a nation, and so on. What people do attempt is the voluntary exit of society, but this too is a lost cause. Individuality is only known relative to the social. Both have to exist for either to exist. Any attempt to exit society must first begin with an awareness of society, a conscious division between one's self and one's surroundings, but this awareness means that the influence of society is already present. Even a person in isolation is still imprinted with the thoughts and language of that person's social setting—if not, that person would not be able to think at all. No individual can ever leave society, he or she can only distance and limit their contact with other persons. Some of us may decide to become hermits, but only after society has given us the social imagination to know that the hermit lifestyle is possible.

Marx's observation that "life is not determined by consciousness, but consciousness by life" was not only an appeal to dialectical materialism, but also to a socialistic understanding of history and philosophy.[30] For Marx "the nature of individuals … depends on the material conditions determining their production," and one of those material conditions, especially in advanced industrialized society, was the inherent socialness of the means of production.[31] What made Marx's socialism "scientific" was that he believed that communism would finally reconcile the increasing socialness of the means of production, being driven by historical and technological forces, and, which served as the basis of society, with a civil structure and philosophy that understood the individual as a social being. Marx's conclusion that "only in community (with others has each) the individual has the means of cultivating his gifts in all directions; only in the community, therefore, is personal freedom possible"[32] was as much as an observation of fact as it was a moral evaluation. The atomization of capitalist society finds justification in liberalism's belief in an abstract individual prior to, or separated, from society.

There was no disagreement with Marx on these points for Bakunin. However, Bakunin's work was more focused on criticizing the idea that social life required the sacrificing of individual liberty in order to attain security. For Bakunin, liberty was an indivisible concept. It existed or it did not; there was no halfway point between liberty and slavery. The reason Bakunin believed this was that he understood liberty as an entirely social affair. The purpose of liberty—the free expression of the individual—could not happen outside of the context of society. For Bakunin "solidarity is not the product of individuality but its mother, and the human individual can be born and develop only in human society."[33] For this reason the idea that a bit of individual liberty could be sacrificed in order to maintain a greater security for society was incomprehensible. The security of society provided the basis for individual liberty.[34]

Both Marx and Bakunin were also in agreement that the freedom inherent in social living was something that could not be extended to the political realm. Whether explicit about it or not, Marx and Bakunin accepted Thomas Paine's understanding on the relationship between society and government that:

> Society is produced by our wants, and government by our wickedness; the former promotes our happiness *positively* by uniting our affections, the latter *negatively* by restraining our vices. The one encourages intercourse, the other creates distinctions. The first is a patron, the last a punisher. ... Society in every state is a blessing, but government even in its best state, is but a necessary evil; in its worst state an intolerable one; for when we suffer, or are exposed to the same miseries *by a government*, which we might expect in a country *without government*, our calamities is heightened by reflecting that we furnish the means by which we suffer.[35]

In the context of a dictatorial monarchy, Paine's distinction between government and society is necessary. The problem with dictatorial regimes—especially modern totalitarian systems—is that they substitute the will of an individual or elite party for the realm of politics, and then elevate this form of a privatized-polity to such a degree that it devours the social realm completely. For example, the Nazi conception of the *Volk*, which assumed that the State was simply an organic expression of a nation, allows for no distinction between politics and society; the State is society, and any rebellion against it amounts to an attack on the people as a whole. Thus, as Hitler as the *Fürher* became the embodiment of the German State, and as the German State became the embodiment of the German *Volk*, any threat to Hitler's power was understood to be a threat to the security of German people as a whole. In this context, Paine's effort to distinguish government and society makes sense. However, Paine does not simply distinguish between political and social realms, he divides them. He sets them up as contrasting forces united in their opposition to each other. For Paine, society is the realm of voluntary association. It "positively" promotes happiness by encouraging sociability among people. In any state it is a "blessing" in the sense that the alternative to society is not government, but an end to sociability, the annihilation of humanity. In contrast, government—as the embodiment of politics—is an inherently violent realm. It is the enforcer, the needed "punisher" that is born of the "wickedness" of humanity. All people should voluntarily obey the social contract, but some do not, and government is needed to force those who refuse. Government can at best be a "necessary evil," in the sense that all forms of coercion, which are engrained in Paine's conception of politics, are evils that humanity should seek to liberate itself from, but tragically cannot due to the follies of our own nature.

The important point to consider with this is liberalism's conception of politics as the power to punish. In the Lockean conception of rights, humans first exist in a state of perfect equality. In this state people have natural rights granted to them by virtue of being born, but this state of nature is inherently unstable due to the human potential to offend. Governments are needed to protect natural rights by punishing criminals and preventing offenses. Essentially, governing for Locke was the science of punishing. What made his political outlook uniquely liberal was his search for proportionality in punishments. Locke sought to make politics a way of restricting violence to a criterion of proportionality. As he explains, "And thus in the state of nature one man comes to power by another; but yet no absolute or arbitrary power, to use a criminal, when he has got him in his hands, according to the passionate heats or boundless extravagance of his own will; but only to retribute to him so far as calm reason and conscience dictate what is proportionate to his transgression."[36] In this view, the protection of natural rights is solely a matter of proportional punishments for individual crimes, and questions of law, which are equated with punishments, are essentially questions of proportionality applied.

The seeds of Marx's and Bakunin's arguments over the dictatorship of the proletariat were planted in this understanding of political action. Both Marx and Bakunin agreed that complete voluntary associations were the goal of humanity, and that political power is essentially the power to use violence. However, Marx believed that the conditions for voluntary association were only possible under communism. Since politics was the superstructure of an economic base, it would first be necessary for certain modes of production to develop before voluntary associations could reign supreme. Until that time the power to punish, the "necessary evil" that is government, could justifiably be used against the capitalist class. Once the capitalists had been annihilated as a class the need for the State and for politics altogether would disappear. In contrast, Bakunin believed that voluntary associations were the means, not the ends, of a new socialist society. For

Bakunin, the "wickedness" of society was the product of the State itself, and, therefore the smashing of the State was the first, not the last, step in creating a socialist world. In placing the blame of society's woes on politics itself, Bakunin stripped government of its "necessity" and exposed it bare as violence.

The problem is that liberalism's theory of political action as proportionate punishments, as a necessary evil, comes with a paradox. If politics is a realm of force and *governing* is defined as the *proper use of violence*, then how do the conditions for that violence become "proper" if the realm of the political only knows the use of force? In other words, if the means in which power is kept in check is through the use of force, then how is it possible to keep political power in check—and ensure that it uses violence only in necessary situations—when governments are defined as those institutions that have a monopoly on the use of force?

Social contract theorists have sought to resolve this paradox by appealing to the threat of revolution. Essentially, violent revolutions are the means in which society has to punish governments for refusing to obey the vertical social contract between the two. In recognition of this, Paine was an adamant defender of the right of people to bear arms, and, without question, access to firearms has been understood to be a right and duty of liberal republicanism. The problem is that the only way a revolution against a government could be possible within liberalism's logic would be if those revolutionary forces were able to use a greater degree of violence than the previous government. Nevertheless, a further monopolizing of force would also mean a more repressive system. The continual concentration of power in order to establish more effective and repressive governments would end up chipping away at the proportionality and personal liberty that is at the foundation of liberalism. Such concentrations inevitably lead to the type of privatized-polity that devours the social realm. Successive revolutions in this mode eliminate the distinction between politics and society and with it the voluntary association so prized by liberalism.

The holding ground for this infinite regression in liberalism is a return to the social contract. But, what is the social contract? It does not exist in any real sense unless it is followed by its members and enforced by some political entity. This argument points to a major problem within liberal social contract theory. At its heart it is essentially a conservative theory. It assumes that there is a metaphysical or natural contract that maintains a particular social order. The truth of its clauses is determined prior to society as a matter of natural or divine law. Absolute freedom is already known in the minds of people and is not something that evolves over the course of history. Revolution is meant in a literal sense, as a return to an original source, a natural state of "perfect equality" for Locke or "perfect liberty" for Rousseau. A belief in such natural states for individuals is completely at odds with a progressive and historical view of social change. Socialism's contribution to the social sciences has been in recognizing that no particular social order can capture the essence of individuals. The entire concept of a social contract, even as a metaphor that is somehow divorced from time and place, is refuted by the great contribution of socialist thinking: that our understanding of humanity is historically and geographically conditioned. New freedoms are constantly being discovered and reinvented with the evolution of society and the continuation of history. They do not exist eternally and are only rediscovered in times of political crisis.

The only way that the progressive nature of revolutions could be explained is if political action is seen as more than a type of punishment. *Government* cannot be defined as merely *that institution which has monopolization on the use of force.* No doubt force is one element of politics, but politics defined purely in these terms ignores how a government gained its monopolization in the first place. Governments have a monopolization of the use of force because they are seen as legitimate. The creation of legitimacy comes prior to the use of force, and, in this way, is more essential to politics than violence. Politics, if it is anything, is the creation of social legitimacy, and this observation breaks down the liberal notion of politics as a realm of coercion. For it is the creation of social legitimacy, more so than an act of violence, that is a matter of shared dialogue and the development of a general agreement on values and actions. Politics is a product of socialization, and not merely a product of violence, and it can even run counter to violence if violent actions, even those by a government, are sufficiently shamed.

Hannah Arendt was one of the few political philosophers to understand this critical point. She recognized the historical confusion between political power and political violence, and insisted on a theoretical distinction between the two. For Arendt, "Violence is by nature instrumental, like all means it always stands in need of guidance through the end it pursues."[37] Violence is always in pursuit of some objective already determined legitimate by society; it needs a justification, and this justification can only come from shared values and norms. Power, however, "needs no justification." It is "inherent in the very existence of political communities."[38] From this observation it is easy to see how the more legitimate a government is—the more the dialogue on its existence is held in common and shared—the more powerful it becomes and the less reliant on force it needs to be. Adherence to law becomes a product of socialization, not an external threat. In this way, government is not necessarily a "necessary evil" that is opposed to the voluntary associations within society but could be the extension of those associations by legitimizing them as a social good.

In a certain sense, both Marx and Bakunin understood this. They both believed in the progressive nature of society, which, as explained above, is problematic for a liberal understanding of politics as a realm of coercion. Both Marx and Bakunin held the conviction that nonviolent voluntary associations would prepare society for its revolutionary reorganization, and thus provide a new legitimacy for socialism. This aspect of their thought actually made the socialist revolution a theoretically less violent affair as compared to the previous bourgeoisie revolutions. Erich Fromm recognized that the idea of,

"political revolution by force is not at all a Marxist idea; it has been the idea of bourgeois society during the last three hundred years ... Marx's theory constituted an important improvement over the middle-class view, an improvement rooted in his whole theory of history. ... Marx saw that political force cannot produce anything for which there has been no preparation in the social and political process."[39]

Indeed, Mao's famous maxim that "political power grows out of the barrel of a gun"[40] may have more to do with the ideas of Locke than Marx. Similarly, in an effort to discourage violence and terrorism among his compatriots, Bakunin advocated for a revolutionary socialism built through changing social relations: "to make a successful revolution, it is necessary to attack conditions and material goods; to destroy property and the State. It will then become unnecessary to destroy men and be condemned to suffer the sure and inevitable reaction which no massacre has ever failed and ever will fail to produce in every society."[41]

What Marx and Bakunin failed to do was systemize these observations in their work. For them the creation of social legitimacy was a question of strategy, not philosophy. What they failed to consider was that their criticism of liberal social contract theory regarding the relationship between the individual and society also should be applied to the relationship between society and government. The assumption of social contract theorists is that social relations can become null and void in the same way a contract can be torn up. Although it is true that specific social ties can be broken off, the sum product of those relations—the manner in which a person is socialized—can never be erased. No person has ever been de-socialized; rather, we are all re-socialized in the context of new settings and institutions. What this means in the context of the relationship between society and government is that societies do not negotiated the terms of their "contracts" with governments any more than individuals negotiate the terms of their "contracts" with society. The relationship between society and government is not binary. There is no contract between the two. Instead, politics is the means in which societies are socialized; complex societies no more enter freely into governments than individuals do into societies. Rather, government becomes the felt need of society once it has reached a degree of complexity beyond the informal relations of kinship and friends. In such situations, people do not *consent* to a government in the same way that they do a contract. Individuals only have the power to actively *consent* or *dissent* to specific policies and decisions of a government, but not to the government as a whole.

The failure of liberal social contract theorists to understand this has created numerous problems in how liberalism understands the relationship between individuals, society, and governments. Again, the foundations of this problem can be found in the work of Locke. Locke seemed unaware of the contradiction that his favoring of majority rule as a method of government was actually incompatible with his theory of government by consent. In *Two Treatises on Government* he wrote, "For when any number of men, by the consent of every individual, made a community, they have thereby made that community one body, with a power to act as one body, which is only by will and determination of the majority."[42] The obvious contraction in these lines is that if the body is based on the consent of "every individual" than why is its "will and determination" simply that of the majority. Any majority implies a minority, but if a minority is not represented in the "will and determination" then it cannot be said to have consented to it. Trying to reconcile the contradiction between consent as individuals and will as a majority has created numerous issues for liberal thinkers of various persuasions. For example, free market libertarians such as Friedrich Hayek have forsaken the majoritarian aspect of Locke's conception of consent of the governed, and believe that the only government that is justified is one based solely on the "consent of every individual." Hayek makes no apologies for his disdain for democracy. He openly acknowledges that democracy is a hostile force to the extreme individualism that he promotes. He is of course right. Democracy does threaten extreme individualism, but that is a problem for extreme individualism, not democracy. A government that is based on the "consent of every individual" is such an anemic institution that it is questionable if it exists as an institution at all. It never rises above the individual interests of its members to form a greater good, and for that reason never demands of its members that they reach for a moral awareness beyond their myopic self-interests. In contrast to free market libertarians, political "realist" such as Reinhold Niebuhr affirms Locke's majoritarian principle, but in doing so forsakes the concept of consent. For them minorities accept the rule of the majority merely because in a democracy the majority's superior people power means that they have superior firepower. For Niebuhr and other "realists," politics, again being thought of as a realm of force, in a democracy is not qualitatively different for that of an authoritarian regime. It is only quantitatively different in the sense that a majority is needed to utilize the State's monopolization of violence. This "realist" view is better described as a cynical view of politics in that it makes no distinction between a genuine democracy and mob rule; it lazily ignores how the checks and balances in a democratic system protect the rights of minorities and how the legal legitimacy of decisions prevents majoritarian domination.

The only way to resolve these issues is to realize that social agreement is a layered phenomenon, and the more complex a society is the more intricate and extreme its layers of agreement become. Eventually the layers of agreement become so intricate that they split into three qualitatively different forms: consent, which is the active agreement to a particular action of government; assent, which is the acceptance to a particular form of government; and attest, which is the conviction that society should be governed at all. Anarchism claims to be an ideology opposed to all forms of government, but in reality most strands of anarchism actually offer clever euphemisms such as "worker's councils," "federation of communes," or "neighborhood and factory committees" that serve as their own anarchist governments. The hope of Marxists and anarchists has always been to somehow provide social governance without actually having a government, at least in name, and, for this reason, they have never been able to shed completely the idea that society does need to be governed. They have just wasted ink by trying to extract the word's meaning without actually having to use it. Only the fringes of anarchism, the extreme individualists of anarcho-capitalism and the eccentric neo-tribalists of anarcho-primitivism, seriously detest the idea of government, and both do so at their own folly. Extreme individualists are oblivious to the reality that the individuality that they so value is only possible through society, and specifically through the complex societies that require governments. It is only in such societies that people have the numerous and varied opportunities for self-expression and personal growth. Government is the reality of such societies, and without it, the extreme individualists would lose the vary individuality that they so desire. Anarcho-primitivists are aware that complex societies require government, and therefore, in their pursuit of a society devoid of government, attack complexity as such. They advocate for a return to tribalism not just in the terms of social structures, but in all areas of life. They are consistent in their approach, but completely lost in their ends. It is true that tribal societies were pre-political societies that existed without governments, but it is not the case that they were at all free. The drive for greater social complexity has been sought as part of, not in opposition to, people's instinct for freedom. The pursuit of a pre-political tribal anarchy would require not only a holocaust of unimaginable proportions, but also a degree of coercion of an unimaginable scale. There would have to be a conscious effort to repress people's urge to improve their tools, to experiment with new artistic forms, and, most importantly, to nurture cosmopolitan desires for stable and diverse communities. Tribal societies that make every effort to maintain their tribal way of life above all else would have to be totalitarian societies. They may be stateless, even nonhierarchical, but they are in no sense free.

Any person who participates in a complex society, that is any society beyond familial and personal relations, *attests* to the concept of a government since such relationships could not exist in the first place unless a government existed to maintain them. From there, individuals can *consent* to specific government actions, but not to government as a form. They can only *assent* to the form of government as an institution, since individuals, on their own, have no means of creating politics and establishing the social legitimacy needed to validate a government as a form. Only society can *consent* to a government, and since government becomes an inevitability of any complex society, societies will only *consent* to those governments capable of managing their complexities. It is never a question *if* social legitimacy will be determined in complex societies, but *how* it will be determined, and societies only withdraw their consent from a specific government once a rival power—an alternative government—exist for that society to invest its consent in. No revolution has ever occurred through resistance alone. It is only through the growth of counter institutions that serve as the focal point of resistance, and specifically a counter government, that society has been able to radically transform itself from one set of social arrangements to another.

The relationship between society and politics, between the people and their government, cannot be reduced to simplistic dualism such as consent versus coercion. Writers such as Arendt and Bookchin were some of the few political philosophers who understood the theoretical importance of this observation. For them the problem with European political philosophy was the conviction that freedom is located solely in the realm of the social and politics was understood as simply the strategic use of the monopoly of violence. Its usefulness is only as a potential protector of freedom, not its creator. In liberalism freedom exists beyond or outside of politics; for civil libertarians it is the private lives of citizens; for free marketers it is private enterprise; and for Marxism and anarchism it is apolitical utopias where the social realm finally conquers politics, instead of the freedom inherent in society being extended through to politics. Both develop their criticism of European political philosophy by relying on another tradition of freedom rooted in the ancient Greek *polis*. The *polis* tradition accepts two aspects of political action that challenge the assumptions of liberal social contract theorists. First, that the relationship between society and government is developmental and dialectical. Politics is, or at least has the potential to be, society aware of itself as society. *Governing* is society in self-reflection, and not necessarily society punishing itself. Second, politics is needed to form the highest degree of ethical living. Society's inherent capacity for individual freedom is extended into political action. The moral practice of freedom is only possible once people step outside their private lives and enter into a public sphere where they must attend to the common good. These two aspects are important, but they are incomplete. The teleological nature of the ancient *polis* tradition provides a backdoor justification for any form of government, no matter how oppressive. Ancient Greek conception of the *polis* does not morally distinguish between the forms of government, and for this reason, all governments can claim to have organically developed from society and be representative of the common good. For this reason, the *polis* tradition needs to be modernized. Murray Bookchin, in his development of Communalism, adds a third aspect to the Greek notion of politics that successfully resolves this issue: an ethic of radical egalitarianism that believes that the ideal form of government is one based on communal democracy. If social legitimacy is derived from a collective dialogue and shared consciousness on proper actions then the strengthening of this legitimacy is only possible through the continual inclusion of others in the process of governance. In this way, the free society is the political society; participation in governance becomes the activity of all, both a duty and a right in one.

The Polis Tradition: A Lost Theory of Politics

Despite the massive amount of literature on the unique experiment in Athenian democracy, very little is still known. The only systematic surviving text of this time period is Aristotle's *The Politics*, and, though offering a conception of politics that differs from liberal social contract theory, it is at times highly critical of democracy. Nevertheless, Aristotle's *The Politics* provides us with a theoretical understanding of two aspects of the *polis* tradition, and its shortcomings explain the need for Communalism to add a third.

First, politics is seen as developing organically out of society as an extension of the private realm or the "household" and not in a binary conflict with society. In stark contrast to Marx's economic determinism, Aristotle understood politics not as part of the "superstructure" of the "base" modes of production within society, but as developing from society through the imperatives of complex social arrangements. As Bookchin explains, for Aristotle "the distinction between the social and the political ... is strikingly processual: the difference is explained by the growth and development of the social into the political, not their polarization and mere succession."[43] Politics was not something people *used* for some purpose as is the case in liberal social contract theory, but as something they *did* as part of who they are as people. The proclamation by Aristotle that man is a "political animal" was because he understood the essence of social living to be directed toward the end *as* politics, not, as Marx and Bakunin thought, the end *of* politics. Society, in so far as it strove for anything, strove to be political. This is an expression of its essential nature. As Aristotle explained, "if the earlier forms of society are natural, so is the state, for it is the end of them, and the nature of a thing is its end. For what each thing is when fully developed, we call its nature."[44]

Aristotle considers politics to be this "end," because politics—unlike individuals merely existing in society—is the only realm that can reach self-sufficiency. "The proof that the state is a creation of nature and prior to the individual is that the individual, when isolated, is not self-sufficing, and therefore he is like a part in relations to the whole."[45] According to Aristotle, there is no such thing as a self-sufficient individual or household. Self-sufficiency can only exist on the social level. Individuals cannot develop themselves except within the context of their relations with others. In the private realm, people can be "sufficient," but not "self-sufficient." Independence is achieved only through increasing our own sense of sociability and interconnectedness. To fully understand Aristotle's point it is necessary to compare humans as "political animals" with those creatures who he sees as having no need for politics: beast and gods. Beast do not form political associations because they have no need for a "self" to reach, while gods do not form political associations, because, being gods, they have no worries of sufficiency. Both, in a certain sense, live outside of society, either because they cannot enjoy its fruits or because they have no need to be nurtured by it in the first place.

From these assumptions Aristotle establishes politics as a moralizing realm, in dramatic contrast to liberalism's conception of politics as a realm of violence. When people act completely outside of politics, in the form of a pre-political anarchy, they act out their most immoral impulses. For Aristotle, political formations are derived from a *koinonia* or a shared communal life, and this shared communal life has an inherent virtue that political formations uphold. For this reason, Aristotle does not consider alliances of a military or economic nature, where cooperation is established to serve a specific goal, or any other contractual relations as being political in nature. The concept of a social contract is a contradiction in terms. Contracts are not formed or adhered to out of a sense of shared virtue, but out of common interests. Once any alliance fails to serve those interests, the compact establishing it is abandoned by its participants.

In this manner, a *polis* conception of politics completely rejects anarchism's goal of establishing a society of free associations that simply operate as a network of alliances as both impractical and immoral. Proudhon, rightfully regarded as the father of modern anarchism, proudly proclaimed that anarchism should replace all laws with contracts under the assumption that society, at its foundation, was simply a series of contracts. All social interactions could be reduced to individual negotiations that could operate fully and freely once governments were swept away. In this conviction, there is only the loosest conception of a *koinonia*, if it even exists there at all. Proudhon never answers the question of who is to enforce these contracts if a party ever decides to break one, and thus leaves him and the rest of anarchism open to the criticism of valuing liberty without ever establishing any means of guaranteeing it.

Second, for Aristotle, politics is the means in which people are able to secure the workings of the "good life" or *eudaimonia*. It is in the difference between "sufficiency" and "self-sufficiency" that Aristotle constructs his conception of "life" and the "good life." As with society and politics, these concepts do not exist as polarities, but as entities with a developmental capacity. One has within it the essential nature of the other, and, through its growth and development, produces the other without vanquishing itself. The development of the social realm into the political realm brings with it a development of "life" into the "good life." This "good life" is not only material, but moral in character. According to Aristotle, the basis of politics—in creating the "good life"—comes from our sense of *paideia*; this is a word that finds a difficult English counterpart. It is often roughly translated into "education" but it is more accurately understood as the "creative integration of the individual into his environment."[46] The idea of *paideia* implies a holistic conception of the individual—a self-awareness of one's social and natural world, and a sense of ethical directionality in changing it. For Aristotle, *paideia* contrasts sharply with the idea of *banausos*. This word is also difficult to find a modern English equivalent, but roughly translates into "mechanically-minded,"[47] implying both a mode of thinking and a description of a person. According to Aristotle, *banausic* learning is the acquisition of knowledge stripped of its inquisitive or virtuous aspects. It is learning simply for the sake of doing without a deeper questioning as to why that thing is being done. Unlike *paidiea, banausos* suggests a complete lack of ethical directionality on the part of the individual; it suggests deferring one's will and being oblivious to one's relationship with the surrounding environment.

For Aristotle, the "good life" is possible only through participation in politics because this is the arena where people are able to mold their *paideia* toward their *arete*—their "excellence in all aspects of life."[48] The experience of politics is what makes us most aware of the world around us. In politics we make decisions not for ourselves but for our entire community. *Arete,* the excellence of our integration into our environment, is only possible through politics because no other activity asks us to widen our perspective more and engage in a broader diversity of views than political participation. We cannot create the "good life" unless we know what "life" is, and politics provides us with the means to know "life."

Aristotle's relationship between "life" and the "good life" is strikingly similar to Marx's own "realm of necessity" and "realm of freedom." Indeed, there is a tremendous amount of crossover between the two in their appreciation of sociability and their recognition of the need to end material scarcity as a precondition for freedom. The major difference is that Marx (and also Bakunin) understood the "realm of freedom" in the terms of freedom to labor as one chooses, outside of political action. The "realm of freedom" is possible once technological advancements eliminate material scarcity; it is a realm that has left the world of toil for hobby and craftsmanship. For Aristotle, the point of leisure is to free people so they are capable of engaging in public life. Sociability and material development only reach their highest potential in a society with political activity. Once our minds and bodies are freed from the burden of toil, they gravitate toward the desire to govern. Hobby and craftsmanship are part of our private lives, they are ways of rejuvenating us for public living, but they are not means of replacing it.

Interestingly enough, this conviction on the part of Aristotle is why he rejected democracy as an ideal form of government. For Aristotle, politics could not occur in any meaningful way unless people had the time and energy to engage in it. During Aristotle's time, such leisure was a privilege for only a small minority. In this way, Aristotle understood democracy as the rule by the caprice and needy. People did not have the knowledge or the means to govern properly because they were too occupied with their own subsistence. The only way Athens had been successful in governing itself is through its slave society and the mixing of common laborers with aristocrats is the polity. The privileged men were able to control the passion of the masses through their superior education, oratorical skills, and by dominating public offices. The necessity for material abundance was considered such an important feature of Aristotle's conception of politics that he included a curious passage in *The Politics* that democracy would still be the rule of the poor, even if the poor were in the minority:

> For the real difference between democracy and oligarchy is poverty and wealth. Wherever men rule by reason of their wealth, whether they be few or many, that is an oligarchy, and where the poor rule, that is a democracy. But as a fact the rich

are few and the poor many; for few are well-to-do, whereas freedom is enjoyed by all, and wealth and freedom are the grounds on which the oligarchical and democratical parties respectively claim power in the state.[49]

To modern, more egalitarian ears, this passage seems perplexing. For Aristotle's time it was quite sensible. Aristotle, like many privileged Greeks, believed in the inevitability of class structure and a stratified society. People were seen as aristocratic by birth, not as they are seen in modern times, where wealth is thought of as resulting from personal merit or social conditions. These antiquated notions of human equality and biological determinism blinded Aristotle to a revolutionary tension between governments of direct democracy and aristocratic and dictatorial forms of governing, or, to put it another way, between communal governments and States.

In *The Politics* Aristotle classifies political systems in terms of their perfect forms. Dictatorship is the ideal form of rule by the one; aristocracy is the ideal form of rule by the few; and democracy is the ideal form of rule by the many. Each system finds its parallel relationship in the household realm where the relationship between the master and slave is that of a dictatorship; the relationship between the husband and wife is an aristocracy; and, the relationship between a man and his friends and brothers is that of a democracy. He then elaborates on the possibly degenerative forms of each: tyranny, oligarchy, and mob rule, respectively. What Aristotle does not discuss is the possibility that one perfect form of government could be the degenerative form of another. For example, Aristotle does not consider the possibility that a dictatorship is perhaps a degenerative form of an aristocracy. The reason this is so is because there is nothing innate in Aristotle's ethical outlook that connects morality to freedom. Indeed, if a society was biologically stratified between classes, races, sexes, and so on, the concept of freedom could be a dangerous one. However, once freedom becomes a question of morality then an entire reclassification of forms of government is needed.

Critics may protest that a *polis* conception of politics is a teleological approach, and therefore, suffers from all the trappings of other forms of teleological thinking that assume ends determine purpose. This is a half-truth that applies specifically to Aristotle. Aristotle's conviction that politics is the end, and therefore the purpose, of society could be used to justify the existence of any government, regardless of how oppressive, as the natural and inevitably end of that particular society. Indeed, in *The Politics* that is much of what Aristotle does. His detached zoological approach in analyzing different governmental systems deemphasizes the ethical dimension that each political system has, as if governments could be selected from in the same way as items of a salad bar rather than carefully theorized and fought for through social struggles. Not only are there a qualitative difference between Aristotle's forms of government, but also radical and explosive tensions between them.

It is often the case that all forms of government that Aristotle lists are described as some type of State where the democracy of ancient Athens is described as a just another "city-state." This is a mistake. Although ancient

Athens definitively had some statist elements, it cannot be understood in the same terms as modern nation-States. As Bookchin explains, "Attic Greek contains no word for state. The term is Latin in origin, and its etymological roots are highly ambiguous. It more properly denotes a person's condition in life ... than a commonwealth or a state in the modern sense of the term. Not until the early sixteenth century ... does the word come to mean a professional civil authority with the power to govern a 'body politic.'"[50] This history is not trivial. As Arendt recognized, what has set the Athenian *polis* apart from other forms of government is the realization that legitimacy was a product of a shared dialogue. For this reason, political action was a matter of collective speech action as opposed to collective violent action. In terms of political power, what mattered most in ancient Athens was the relevance of collective meaning. According to Arendt, "wherever the relevance of speech is at stake, matters become political by definition, for speech is what makes man a political being"[51] while sheer violence is always "mute, and for this reason violence alone can never be great."[52] In this way, the Athenians can be credited with the understanding of politics as democratic governance.[53]

The emphasis on shared dialogue over violence as the source of social legitimacy is counter to the hierarchical forms of organization that are ingrained into all State structures. Shared dialogue is only possible if there is a degree of equality among conversing members. If politics really is the dialectical self-reflection of society, in Hegelian terms, a "doing away with and coming-into-being" of society, then social freedom is only possible in a political system that aims for the highest level of shared dialogue. In this way, communal democracy is the form of politics in which politics becomes aware of itself *as politics*.

The State is a structural form of domination and violence that works against the dialectical development of the socialrealm into the political realm. In Platonic terms, it is a social *eristic*[54]—a means in which the development of society is stifled and society is turned against itself. Instead of politics being a "doing away with and coming into" it becomes a "doing away with *as* a coming into."Not all things brought forth through a dialectical synthesis are necessarily part of its logical development, and not all political formations are the inevitable end of society. They are only one possibility within a range of ends that a society could produce. The State may rise out of politics, but it is not "the truth" of politics. If anything, States are politics inconsistent with itself.

Communalism distinguishes itself from ancient *polis* theory of politics by adding an important division between politics and statecraft. Statecraft is a form of alienated politics, where ruler and ruled, governor and governed, politician and constituent are divided rather than synthesized into the greater whole of citizenship. In this division statecraft becomes the deformed practice of politics. It is politics without its *paideia*; it is a *banausos* politics that understands all actions as justified, regardless of moral consequences, as long as they can serve the interests of the State. The idea that political action and moral action would be at all separated when the purpose of politics is to serve the "good life" means that the "politics" of the State is not an authentic form of governance. Rather, it is a parasitic zombie form of government that lumbers along, feeding on society without nurturing it. Politics cannot be realized through the various forms of hierarchy and modes of repression that are at the essence of all statists governments. The State cannot be understood on its own terms, but politics can; or, rather, political power can only be understood through the lens of democratic governance, meaning democracy is the essence of politics and not just one of its possible forms.

A New Leftwing Generation

The proclamation that "we are the 99%" by the Occupy Wall Street movement has been the movement's most significant rallying cry. It is important to remember that this expression itself was recognized, even by the most sectarian participants of the movement, as point of discussion and not as a basis for identity. Some participants even added the trailing phrase "and this is for the 100%," implying a political victory through absorption, not annihilation. The idea that the "99%" has within its reach the power to create a world that truly embraces "100%" of humanity is obviously appealing. But, in order to make this world a reality, a coherent and focused politics for the "99%" must be formed. This has not occurred. As mentioned before, the general assemblies did embody the act of collective dialogue, but they failed to realize a good that was greater than the sum of its participants. The general assemblies may have given its participants a sense of liberty, in the sense that they provided them some control over the decisions in running the encampments, but they never created any real freedom. As members of Occupy Wall Street, the activists remained sufficient beings, not self-sufficient beings that were able to realize their greatest potential through their interconnectedness with others.

At the root of this failure is an inability of activists to appreciate the need for political power. The traditions of Marxism and anarchism have locked revolutionary social movements into an irrational utopianism that denies the significances of politics in creating the good life; the realization of a socialist society has either been passively entrusted to specialists, who will "wither away" the State after seizing it, or frantically ascribed to the masses who will smash all politics through their leaderless spontaneity. Neither will work. A socialist society can only be created through a political society. Political power must be created through the development of institutions that truly embody the principles of democracy. This demands that activists recognize that it is the institution, democratically organized, that is the source of freedom, not individuals or vanguard elites.

The most important lesson of the Occupy Wall Street movement is the realization that the general assemblies were a nascent *polis* in the Arendtian sense: "the organization of the people as it arises out of acting and speaking together."[55] This practice of "acting and speaking together" makes politics a communal rather than hierarchical affair. Politics becomes a good—in so far as social living is a good—in and of itself, rather than being an evil that needs to be proportionally applied in order to be made into a good. Strengthening the general assemblies so that they were able to become actual institutions, and not merely gatherings for individuals, should have been Occupy Wall Street's main objective. The liberation of individuals is only possible through the creation of liberating institutions, and not the other way around.

This reorientation of radical activism towards institution building is just one of the many aspects that call for a new type of leftwing racialism. The first generation of Leftism began in the mid-nineteenth century with the republican revolutions that swept across Europe and ended with the Second World War. This generation, referred to as the Old Left, defined itself within the context of industrialization. Revolutionary movements at this time focused mainly on the struggles of the working class in Europe and North America. The center for reform and resistance was the workplace and the main agent of social change was the industrial proletariat. The Old Left sought a proletarian socialism that could reconcile the radical social disjunctions created by the industrial revolution. In the context of the extreme social and technological changes that were occurring under industrialism, much of this made sense. However, once the rapidity of the industrial transformation slowed the shortsightedness of these beliefs became evident. Within the Old Left, there was token rhetoric to an "international working class," but a close examination of the phrased revealed it to be a contradiction. The majority of the world's downtrodden were not industrial proletarians, but peasants still locked in a rural poverty and feudal social system. Proletarian socialism had little meaning for them. Also, the elevating of workers as revolutionary agents not only minimized the revolutionary work that was underway under various other identities (such as women, ethnic minorities, youth, and so on), but also blinded radicals to the reactionary potential of the working class. The nearly universal support for the First World War, even among many radical socialists and anarchists, showed how the working classes were just as likely to adopt a regressive national consciousness opposed to a revolutionary class consciousness.

The end of the Second World War brought in a truly new world order that the theoretical tools of the Old Left were unable to comprehend. The State guaranteed a degree of public welfare and took on a greater role in initiating and directing technological innovation. The world had started to become truly global, both in the sense of world imperialism and in the sense of global governance. State sovereignty altered itself in the context of new institutions like the United Nations. And, the great strides of women, ethnic minorities, youth, and other marginalized groups revealed that a socialist society was not a prerequisite for the liberation of these groups.

These dramatic changes lead to the birth of the New Left. The New Left was an attempt to move the revolutionary struggle beyond the context of industrialism. The most important contribution of the New Left has been in opening up our collective consciousness to issues of feminism, multiculturalism, third world movements, queer theory, and the environment, and, in doing so, has shown us the multiple ways in which various forms of oppression operate. The New Left brought to light new centers of social struggle—such as the family, the school, the neighborhood, the environment, and cultural and ethnic ties—all of which have competed with and altered the workplace as the primary organizing venue. In addition, the New Left was far more cognizant of global affairs and sensitive to the liberation of people living under the imperialist heel of Europe and North America. The Vietnam War and the treatment of colonized nations practically defined the essential character of the New Left. Its members understood the Cold War in a global context that the only a few members of the Old Left did for the First and Second World Wars. However, though the New Left has made the revolutionary movements more inclusive and more global, the revolutions of the New Left were changes in the social realm. It failed to offer any coherent political alternative to States. Within the New Left, the proletarian socialism of the Old Left bifurcated. The Marxists, under the influence of Maoism, replaced proletarian socialism with third world nationalism, and morphed the universal struggle against capitalism to the specific struggles of leaders in the third world to break with the legacy of imperialism and modernize their economies. In contrast, the anarchists created their own bohemian socialism that reduced resistance to capitalism to a rejection of consumerism, and advocated for various lifestyle changes as a substitute for political organizing. Both adopted the cry of "participatory democracy," but offering elaborate apologies for brutal dictators in the developing world or celebrating the "subversive" lifestyle of freewheeling individuals really has nothing to do with democracy—participatory or otherwise. For this reason, despite its great gains in social inclusion, the New Left failed.

Today, we live in a world far more globalized than ever before. The major existential crisis facing the world today is not the outbreak of a world war, but the continual environmental destruction caused by market failures in the developed world and the anarchical race of developing nations to modernize their economies. At the same time, the nation-State has dramatically altered as an institution. National independence as become equated with participation within the United Nations. The isolationist sovereignty of nation-States has given way to an integrationist sovereignty, and thus, new, more global forms of statecraft have emerged. Meanwhile, the global economy has gone through important structural changes that make previous analyses of capitalism obsolete. The social welfare that States originally provided in the post-World War II era has been gutted. Neoliberal economics reigns supreme, but only halfheartedly. At the same time States have peeled back their social welfare programs they have taken on an even greater role in developing new technologies. Previous leftwing analyses have only given us the faintest understanding of how to comprehend these changes, and even less of it provides answers into how to utilize these changes for mobilizing for a better world.

This means that there exists a possibility and a need for a New, New Left that can build on the best elements of the past, consolidate them into radical forms of political action, and push them forward to a better tomorrow. This new generation of leftwing activism can only realize itself by offering a theoretically coherent vision of politics—one that shrugs off the trappings of both Marxism and anarchism—and practices this vision in a manner that is realistic enough to be relevant, but imaginative enough to be revolutionary.Communalism, in its appreciation for politics, must play a preeminent role in making this happen. If Marxism sought to seize political power and the State and anarchism sought to abolish political power and the State, and both have failed, then our best hope lies with Communalism's advocacy to seize political power in order to smash the State. Our greatest prospect for winning a socialist society is the creation of a political society, the formation of a global confederation of communal governments, a directly democratic world government that can abolish all nation-States. After over a century and a half of attempts by the Left to realize the socialist's dreams through either State violence or a rejection of political action, it might be our only option left. The Occupy Wall Street movement has given us a glimmer of this possibility. Transforming those glimmers into sparks and eventual into flames means being realistic of the failures of yesterday and hopeful about the potential for tomorrow; it is only through this balancing of realism and hope that we are ever able to push forward into better futures.

Notes

1 Karl Marx, "The German Ideology." In Robert C. Tucker, ed., *The Marx-Engels Reader*, 2nd Edition (New York: W.W. Norton & Company 1978), 160.

2 *ibid*, 161.

3 *ibid*, 161.

4 Robert M. Cutler, "Introduction," in Robert M. Cutler, ed., *The Basic Bakunin: Writings 1869-1871* (New York: Prometheus Books 1992), 21.

5 Karl Marx, "Contributions to the Critique of Hegel's Philosophy of Right." In Tucker, ed., *The Marx-Engels Reader*, 20.

6 *ibid*, 20, emphasis in original.

7 Karl Marx, "Manifesto of the Communist Party." In Tucker, ed., *The Marx-Engels Reader*, 490.

8 Karl Marx, "Address of the Central Committee to the Communist League." In Tucker, ed., *The Marx-Engels Reader*, 507.

9 Karl Marx, "The Civil War in France." In Tucker, ed., *The Marx-Engels Reader*, 633.

10 *ibid*, 632.

11 For an elaboration of this critique of Marx see Murray Bookchin, *Remaking Society: Pathways to a Green Future* (Boston: Black Rose Books, 1990).

12 Ernest Gellner, "Economic Interpretations of History." In John Eatwell and Murray Milgate, ed., Marxian Economics: The New Palgrave (New York: Palgrave Macmillan 1990), 155.

13 Vladimir Lenin, "The State and Revolution." In Robert C. Tucker, ed., *The Lenin Anthology* (New York: W.W. Norton & Company 1975), 353.

14 Karl Marx, "Capital, Volume Three." In Tucker, ed., *The Marx-Engels Reader*, 441.

15 Marx, "The German Ideology," 160.

16 Erich Fromm, *Marx's Concept of Man* (New York: Frederick Ungar Publishing, 1966), 24.

17 Michael Bakunin, "The International and Marx." In Sam Dolgoff, ed., *Bakunin on Anarchy* (Montreal: Vintage Books, 1980), 318.

18 Frank T. Fitzgerald, *The Cuban Revolution in Crisis: From Managing Socialism to Managing Survival* (New York: Monthly Review Press, 1994), 50.

19 Michael Bakunin, "Federalism, Socialism, Anti-Theologism." In Dolgoff, ed., *Bakunin on Anarchy,* 104-105.

20 Michael Bakunin, "The Paris Commune and the Idea of the State." In Dolgoff, ed., *Bakunin on Anarchy,* 263.

21 *ibid.*

22 Mikhail Bakunin, "Federalism, Socialism, Anti-Theologism." In Dolgoff ed., *Bakunin on Anarchy*, 142.

23 Mikhail Bakunin, "The Policy of the International." In Cutler, ed., *The Basic Bakunin*, 210, note 35.

24 Sam Dolgoff, "The Anarchism of Micheal Bakunin." In Dolgoff, ed., *Bakunin on Anarchy,* 74.

25 Paul Avrich, "Preface" to Dolgoff, ed., *Bakunin on Anarchy,* xix.

26 Cutler, "Introduction." in Cutler, ed., *The Basic Bakunin*, 21.

27 Murray Bookchin, "The Communalist Project," *Harbinger: A Journal of Social Ecology* (2003), 21, emphasis in original.

28 Bakunin, "The Organization of the International," 141, emphasis in original.

29 The exception is Rousseau whose theory of the "general will" collapses both the horizontal and vertical elements of the social contract into one. This unique characteristic of Rousseau's own political thinking does rightfully make him both a forefather

of fascism and anarchism; whereas anarchism interpreted his
"general will" in its horizontal manifestation, fascism interpreted
it in its vertical sense. Both have some truth in their argument,
but Rousseau's "general will"—true to his romantic impulse and
noble savage motif—is a chimera that attempts to mesh the social
informalities and egalitarianism of tribal society with the complexities
of a nation-state, and that is an impossible social creation.

30 Marx, "The German Ideology," 155.

31 *ibid,* 150.

32 *ibid,* 197.

33 Bakunin, "All-Round Education." In Cutler, ed., *The Basic
    Bakunin,* 121.

34 Bakunin was also not convinced by the argument by social contract
    theorists that the conflicting individual interests required a strong
    State to repress conflicts for the greater good. The existence
    of society itself suggested a potential for the harmonization of
    individual interests. For Bakunin, conflict was the product, not the
    basis, of social hierarchies. The elimination of the State and class
    rule meant that a harmonization of interests would be realized.

35 Thomas Paine, *Common Sense,* (Minneola: Dover Thrift,1997), 2-3,
    emphasis in original.

36 John Locke, "Second Treatise on Civil Government." In John
    Somerville and Ronald E. Santoni Benite, eds., *Social and Political
    Philosophy* (New York: Anchor Books, 1963), 171.

37 Hannah Arendt, *On Violence* (San Diego: Harcourt Brace, 1970), 51.

38 *ibid,* 52.

39 Fromm, *Marx's Concept of Man,* 23.

40 Mao Tse-Tung, *Quotations From Chairman* (Peking: Foreign
    Language Press, 1966), 61.

41 Michael Bakunin, "The Program of the International Brotherhood." In Dolgoff, ed., *Bakunin on Anarchy*, 151.

42 John Locke, "Second Treatise on Civil Government," 179.

43 Murray Bookchin, *Urbanization Without Cities: The Rise and Decline of Citizenship* (Montréal: Black Rose Books, 1992), 39.

44 Aristotle, *Politics and Poetics*, translated by Benjamin Jowett and S. H. Butcher (New York: The Heritage Press), 8.

45 *ibid*, 4.

46 Bookchin, *Urbanization Without Cities*, 59.

47 For more on the concept of "mechanically-minded" see Philip Wheelwright, ed., *Aristotle* (New York: The Odyssey Press, 1951), 217 footnote 5 and 285 footnote 2.

48 Bookchin, *Urbanization Without Cities*, 59.

49 Aristotle, *Politics and Poetics*. 93.

50 Bookchin, *Urbanization Without Cities*, 33-34.

51 Hannah Arendt, *The Human Condition* (Chicago: University of Chicago Press, 1989), 3.

52 *ibid*, 26.

53 For more on how Athens created politics see Bookchin, *Urbanization Without Cities*.

54 The idea of eristic comes from Plato's notion of dialectics. Plato saw the importance of dialectics as a "method" for coming to true through argumentation, and discouraged the Heraclitean notion that all things existed in constant flux, because he feared falling into nihilism. For Plato, thought was the only thing abstract enough to the continuous and constant changes of dialectical development, but thought too could be corrupted. Plato favored that only "good men" use dialectical arguments, because its process of refutation and negation could strip the philosopher of all morality. According to Plato for

untrained philosophers a dialectical argument could easily become an eristic. Instead of the purpose of discussion being a process of coming to greater truth, it becomes an art of winning arguments; a process that is fundamentally antilogical. See Richard Robinson, *Plato's Earlier Dialectic* (Oxford: Oxford University Press, 1966).

55 Arendt, *The Human Condition*, 198.

Made in the USA
Monee, IL
07 July 2026

56547992R00039